Systems

Book One
Exploration, Culture, and Ecology

Differentiated Curriculum
for
Fourth Grade

ISBN 978-1-59363-270-0

To order, please contact us at
http://www.prufrock.com

Prufrock Press' Differentiated Curriculum Kits provide hands-on, discovery-based, research-oriented activities that are cross-curricular. Prufrock curriculum guides save valuable time, are easy to use, and are highly effective. Each unit begins with a pre-assessment and ends with a post-assessment, so growth and progress can be tracked. Lessons are tied to National and Texas State Standards, freeing teachers to spend more time with students. Each activity is a complete lesson with a focus, closure, extension(s), and suggested assessment opportunities. Differentiated strategies are also identified in every lesson. The evaluation tools are authentic, requiring students to demonstrate knowledge by practical application. Rubrics are provided to help with assessment.

We recognize that one activity cannot reach every student at every ability level, so suggestions are given for modifications. Please feel free to modify activities as needed.

Prufrock curricula are based on conceptual themes. By using abstract words such as *wonders, changes, structures*, and *powers*, the topics are broad, universal, and timeless. Research proves that conceptual learning helps bridge the disciplines requiring higher-order thinking, which in turn leads to meaningful understanding.

Come explore the world of Systems...

Systems Book 1 contains the following subtopics:
Exploration, Culture, and Ecology

What would happen if we had automobiles, but no roads? Light bulbs, but no electricity? Our world functions smoothly when systems are in place. Transportation, health care, and education are all organized into systems we depend upon daily. Students will discover the importance of systems and the consequences when one part of a system is removed or does not function properly. Ecosystems, monetary systems, and settlement are examined as students research to build upon prior knowledge to predict future trends in technology, education, and economics. Once students appreciate the value of systems in their lives today, they will begin creating the innovative systems of the future.

Please see our other *Systems Trilogy* titles:
Systems Book 2: Settlement, Currency, and Measurement
Systems Book 3: Economics, Climate, and Comparisons

Acknowledgements

We would like to credit Sandra N. Kaplan, Javits Projects, University of Southern California, for the use of the Depth and Complexity Dimensions in our materials.

A special thank you to Suzy Hagar, Executive Director for Advanced Academic Services in the Carrollton-Farmers Branch Independent School District, for project development advice, suggestions, and support.

Written by: Debbie Keiser, Sarah Wolfinsohn, and Brenda McGee
Cover Design by: Brandon Bolt
Inside Illustrations by: Brandon Bolt
Edited by: Debbie Keiser, Brenda McGee, and Linda Triska

NOTE

The Web sites in this curriculum were working and age-appropriate at the time of publication, but Prufrock Press has no control over any subsequent changes.

Table of Contents

Checklists

Notes

_____

_____

_____

_____

_____

_____

_____

_____

_____

_____

_____

_____

_____

_____

_____

_____

_____

_____

_____

Unit Planner

Concept: Systems Book 1
Grade level: 4
Length of Time: 40+ hours

Exploration
- solar system
- electricity
- metric system

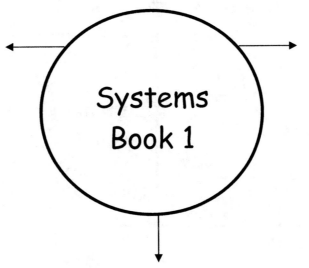

Systems Book 1

Culture
- language
- state characteristics
- learning a trade
- transportation
- celebrations
- family history

Ecology
- water cycle
- adaptation
- mass extinction

Unit Overview

Systems are a means of organizing and categorizing information, improving the quality of life and also breaking things down into a common denominator. In this curriculum students will discover weather systems, transportation systems, electrical systems, and natural systems such as the water cycle and food chain. Systems behind culture and traditions will be uncovered. The relationships between different kinds of systems will also be explored.

Enduring Understandings and Generalizations

Systems may provide a way to organize and categorize things.

Systems may provide a common denominator for people to understand many topics.

Systems may improve the quality of life for some people.

The word systems, has many meanings.

Guiding Questions for *Systems Book 1*

Guiding questions are the factual (F), conceptual (C), and philosophical (P) questions addressed in the curriculum. These are the questions students should be able to answer after completing the activities in this curriculum.

(F) What is a solar system?

(F) How many planets are in our solar system?

(F) What are the differences between a planet and a star?

(F) Who was Louis Braille?

(F) How do discoveries and inventions differ?

(F) What is the metric system?

(F) What is meant by learning a trade?

(F) How has the railroad changed our culture?

(F) What aspects of a culture can be found in traditional celebrations?

(F) What family stories are passed down from generation to generation in your family?

(F) What is the drawback to only using an oral history to remember family stories?

(F) What are the stages of the water cycle?

(F) What are the roles of the producers, consumers and decomposers in a food chain?

(F) What is weather?

(F) What is an ecosystem?

(F) What is an adaptation?

(F) What factors may have contributed to the mass extinction of the dinosaurs?

(C) How has the Braille system helped blind people improve their quality of life?

(C) How has electricity affected our lives?

(C) Why does each state have unique characteristics?

(C) Why do some people feel that western expansion was detrimental?

(C) Why do people strive to maintain traditional celebrations?

(C) Why is the sun critical to the water cycle?

(C) How does the loss of a member in a food chain impact the entire food chain?

(C) How do climate and weather systems affect the populations of towns in the United States?

(C) If an ecosystem changes, what determines if an organism survives?

(C) Why should we care how the dinosaurs became extinct?

(C) Why is passing down a trade a cultural tradition in Korea?

(P) Should every country in the world use the metric system?

F= factual question
C= conceptual question
P= philosophical question

Notes

_____

_____

_____

_____

_____

_____

_____

_____

_____

_____

_____

_____

_____

_____

_____

Activity 1 — Pre-Assessment

Gifted Strategies
Knowledge and Skills
- Categorizing
- Attributes

Multiple Perspectives
- Brainstorming

Instructional Materials
- 1 copy of Attachment 5 per pair of students
- journal for each student (a single-subject spiral works well, or students can create journals by stapling 50 sheets of notebook paper between two sheets of construction paper in a book fashion)

Preparation
Cut apart the word cards on Attachment 5 before class. Keep the sets of word cards separated. Use a paper clip to hold each set together.

A. Ask students to form pairs. Present each pair with a set of word cards.

B. Have students separate the cards into three categories. Students can create their own categories or select three words from their word cards to become category headings.

C. Distribute journals. Explain that students will record all their ideas and activities related to the study of systems. Explain process record to students. Here is a short explanation you can use.

A process record is a written record of the work you have done. Your journals will serve as a good place to record information during this unit of study. You will use your journals to record research, ideas, generalizations, and so forth. Your process record will be a reflection of what you are learning. Whenever you brainstorm, perform an experiment, or need a place to record information, you will do so in your journals.

> ### Teacher Tip
> **Bloom's Taxonomy** of learning objectives is the easiest and one of the best ways to **differentiate**. Use your favorite search engine to find and print a chart to keep close. Move your students up the taxonomy by changing your verbs at the **Knowledge, Comprehension, Application, Analysis, Synthesis,** and **Evaluation** levels.

D. Remind students that their journals should be neat. Tell them a simple way to do this is to always begin writing for new assignments on the next clean page in their journals. They should date the top of the page and complete the task on that page.

E. Have students record their categorizing in their journals.

F. Invite students to share their results with the class.

G. Save journal responses for comparison at the end of the *Systems* curriculum.

Notes

_____

_____

_____

_____

_____

_____

_____

_____

_____

_____

_____

_____

_____

_____

_____

_____

_____

_____

Activity 2 — Beyond Earth

Differentiation Strategies

Analysis and Synthesis
- Generalizations
- Critical Thinking

Multiple Perspectives
- Inquiry
- Evaluate Situations

Methodology and Use of Resources
- Uses Technological Media
- Note Taking

Enduring Understanding

Systems may provide a common denominator for people to understand many topics.

Guiding Questions

(F) What is a solar system?
(F) How many planets are in our solar system?
(F) What is the difference between a planet and a star?

Instructional Materials
- computer with Internet access
- 5 pieces of chart paper
- 1 copy of Attachment 6 per student
- books about space, space exploration, and the moon

Background Information

Earth is a small planet in a solar system that is a part of the Milky Way galaxy. A **galaxy** is a group of stars and planets that are a part of the larger universe. The **universe** is all the discovered and undiscovered space that surrounds Earth.

A **solar system** consists of a sun and the planets, asteroids, and comets revolving around it. The nine planets in our solar system revolve around the sun in elliptical patterns. **Gravity** is the greatest force in the universe. The gravitational pull of the sun causes the planets to revolve around it.

Many planets in our solar system have natural satellites orbiting them called moons. Only three planets do not have at least one moon.

Note

The Web sites in this curriculum were working and age-appropriate at the time of publication, but Prufrock Press has no control over any subsequent changes.

Preparation

Visit www.yahooligans.com to locate safe Web sites for students to use for research.

Write each of the following questions on a piece of chart paper and place the papers around the room.
- What are the names of the planets in our solar system?
- What is the Milky Way?
- Why do stars twinkle?
- What are the differences between a planet and a star?
- Why is it called a solar system?

A. Divide students into five groups and have them answer the question on each piece of chart paper. Tell them to make good guesses if they do not know the answer. Discuss the answers before each group rotates to the next question.

B. Distribute copies of Attachment 6. Have students use information from the following Web site to help them answer the questions. As always, please preview the site before allowing student access.
http://www.enchantedlearning.com/subjects/astronomy/planets/

Answers
1. 57 million miles
2. 90°F
3. 225 Earth days
4. a. 486 days
   b. about 1 1/3 years
5. 4,200 miles
6. nearly 17 days
7. Jupiter, Saturn, and Neptune
8. Saturn
9. Pluto

C. Challenge students to brainstorm questions about space, which will be starting points for more research about our solar system. Here are some questions to get students started:
- What is a black hole?
- What causes the moon to change shape every month?
- Why do solar and lunar eclipses occur?
- How do the sun and moon cause the tides in our oceans?
- Is there life on other planets?
- Can we live on other planets?
- Are there other solar systems like ours?
- What color are stars?

D. Encourage pairs of students to select a question to research and give a presentation. Remind students to use their journals as a process record, keeping track of the research they do and recording the first drafts of their reports.

E. Share the rubrics on Attachments 1 and 2, explaining that reports and presentations will be evaluated using these forms. Tell students as they research and plan their presentations that they can use the information on the rubrics to work toward a particular score. Explain the scoring system.

F. When students are ready to combine their research into a presentation, encourage them to select a unique way to present their work. Here are a few ideas to get them thinking:
- Write a training manual for a new planetarium tour guide.
- Write a science fiction story using the elements of a story (characters, setting, plot, climax, resolution, ending) that conveys the answer to the question.
- Create a scale model of the heavenly body and a written report describing what research was completed and what was learned while answering the question.
- Create and present an illustrated time line showing a system of change. (i.e., phases of the moon, the tilt of the Earth on its axis to show the different seasons, the orbit of Earth around the Sun, etc.)
- Write and direct a television commercial advertising a new astronomy college and use the research to show prospective students what they can learn. There should be an element of persuasion with this choice as well.

G. Here are more Web sites for students to use when researching. As always, please preview the sites before allowing student access:
- **http://starchild.gsfc.nasa.gov/docs/StarChild/StarChild.html**
- **http://amazing-space.stsci.edu/**
- **http://www.jpl.nasa.gov/galileo/**
- **http://www.nsip.net/index.cfm**

H. Invite students to present their work to the class. Encourage students to take notes on each presentation.

Closure

A. Challenge students to write three generalizations in their journals about space using the following guidelines:
- The first generalization should be about how the information in one of the presentations directly affects Earth. For example: The tilt of the Earth on its axis directly affects the surface temperature of Earth.
- The second generalization should tie two of the presentations together. For example: Earth's orbit is influenced by the sun.
- The third generalization should be about their own presentations. For example: The effects of solar flares are not totally understood.

B. Initiate a discussion about why we call a solar system a solar system. Ask students why the word *system* is used.

Extensions

A. Encourage students to visit the following Web site to discover opportunities to see the International Space Station in the night sky. As always, please preview any sites before allowing student access:

http://spaceflight.nasa.gov/realdata/sightings/SSapplications/Post/SightingData/sighting_index.html

B. Encourage students to create a class Web site about our solar system. Enlist a technology specialist at your school to help. Have students take digital photos of their visuals and post their reports to the site. As students work further in their studies of systems, have them add their new information to the site.

Assessment

A. Use Attachments 1 and 2 to assess student reports and presentations. Use the rubric on Attachment 3 to assess generalizations.

B. Use the answer key after step B to check the answers on Attachment 6. Evaluate the questions created on Attachment 6 based on depth and difficulty.

Notes

_____

_____

_____

_____

_____

_____

_____

_____

_____

_____

_____

_____

Activity 3 — Language Systems

Differentiation Strategies

Knowledge and Skills
- Attributes
- Classifying

Analysis and Synthesis
- Generalizations
- Inferences
- Evaluate Situations

Communication
- Uses Technological Media
- Research

Enduring Understanding
Systems may improve the quality of life for some people.

Guiding Questions
(F) Who was Louis Braille?
(C) How has the Braille system helped blind people improve their quality of life?

Instructional Materials
- computer with Internet access
- biographies of Helen Keller and Louis Braille
- journals

Background Information

Louis Braille is often credited with inventing the reading system for blind people called Braille. This system uses raised dots in patterns on a page. However, Braille's invention was actually an innovation of the work of French Army Captain Charles Barbier de la Serre. He invented a special code of raised dots to be passed through the trenches at night and read by touch. Barbier visited the school Braille attended, and Braille quickly decided that this sort of language might be useful for blind people. He eventually developed a letter system based on six raised dots than was much simpler that the original system of 12 dots. Unfortunately, Braille died before the new system caught on.

A. Ask students to write in their journals about other languages they know. They may write words they know or share experiences about traveling in other countries. Ask **multilingual** students to count to 10 or say the days of the week in another language.

B. Have students describe in their journals how written and spoken languages are systems. Invite students to share their responses.

C. Ask students to identify the system blind people use to read and write. (Braille) Have students share what they know about Louis Braille and the writing system he developed. Then share the Background Information with students.

D. Tell students they will research Louis Braille's life, the implementation of the Braille system, and the life of Helen Keller, a person who was blind and deaf. Tell students they will put together a time line showing the invention, innovation, and development of the Braille system and connect it to Keller's life. Explain that the Presentation Rubric on Attachment 2 will be used to assess this assignment. Provide the following Web sites for research. As always, please preview all sites before allowing student access:

- **http://www.rnib.org.uk/wesupply/fctsheet/braille.htm**
- **http://www.duxburysystems.com/braille.asp**
- **http://www.his.com/~pshapiro/braille.html**
- **http://www.rnib.org.uk/wesupply/fctsheet/keller.htm**
- **http://www.afb.org/info_document_view.asp?documentid=1350**

E. Have students research American Sign Language and Braille using the following Web sites. Encourage students to use information from these sites in their time lines.
- **http://www.factmonster.com/ipka/A0200808.html**
- **http://www.infoplease.com/ipa/A0200808.html**

F. Have students present their time lines to the class. Encourage students to research other innovations for people who do not see or hear well. Students may wish to research and create an innovation to help people with physical challenges. Be sure to provide guidance as students use the Internet for research.

Closure

A. Have students reflect in their journals what they learned about the development of the Braille system and how it affected people all over the world.

B. Invite students to write three generalizations about the material in their presentations. Sample generalizations:
- The invention of the Braille system enabled blind people to become more independent.
- Being blind and deaf, Helen Keller had to work extra hard to succeed.

Extensions

A. Use the blank rubric on Attachment 4 to create a new evaluation rubric to evaluate new languages created by students in the following step of the Extension activity. Enlist the help of students to help you decide what to evaluate. Here are some possible criteria: creativity, simplicity, and ease of teaching others. Have students fill in the blank rubric and be sure everyone understands the guidelines before moving on.

> ### Teacher Tip
> Rubrics are an effective assessment tool in evaluating student performance in areas which are complex and vague. By involving students in the creation of the rubric, the students take more responsibility for their own learning.

B. Have students complete the Biography Tic-Tac-Toe on Attachment 12.

C. Challenge students to design a new way to communicate. It can be a new verbal or written language, or a nonverbal body language such as blinking a certain way. To give students an idea of how to create a new language, have them visit the following PBS Web site. As always, please preview all sites before allowing students access. **http://pbskids.org/cgi-registry/zoom/ubbidubbi.cgi**

D. Have students work together in pairs to create a new language and prepare a simple lesson to teach their language to the class.

E. Invite students to present their new languages. Have students evaluate each new language using the rubric they created earlier.

F. Award prizes for the new languages such as most original, creative, humorous, and complex. Be sure each team receives a prize.

G. Have students visit the following Web site to learn to say *hello* in many languages. **http://www.ipl.org/div/kidspace/hello/index.html**

Assessment
Use Attachment 2 to evaluate the time line presentations.

Notes

_____

_____

_____

_____

_____

_____

_____

_____

_____

_____

_____

Activity 4 — Electric Systems

Differentiation Strategies
Knowledge and Skills
- Attributes
- Categorizing
- Research

Analysis and Synthesis
- SCAMPER
- Drawing Conclusions
- Generalizations

Enduring Understanding
Systems may improve the quality of life for some people.

Guiding Questions
(F) How do discoveries and inventions differ?
(C) How has electricity affected our lives?

Instructional Materials
- several flashlights that can be disassembled and reassembled
- 1 working string of holiday lights (See Preparation.)
- (6) 9-volt batteries
- duct tape
- wire strippers
- wire cutters
- several items to test the ability to conduct electricity (cotton ball, penny, scissors, ruler, water, paper clip, etc.)
- copies of Attachments 7 and 8 (as needed)
- computer with Internet access

Optional:
- 1 large, used box
- several feet of insulated wire

Background Information
A **discovery** is an existing thing that seems new because someone found it for the first time. An **invention** is a new thing created by someone. An **innovation** takes place when someone adds to an invention or combines it with something else.

Simple machines were invented thousands of years ago. Most things with moving parts inside are based on the six simple machines: wheel and axle, pulley, inclined plane, wedge, gears, and levers. This means most things being developed today are not inventions, but innovations.

The flashlight is an innovation. It is made of a **circuit** containing a light bulb (thank you, Thomas Edison), a conductor made of wire (thank you, Benjamin Franklin), and a plastic or metal casing. The flashlight is the result of hard work by many inventors and innovators.

A **conductor** is a material that conducts electricity, such as wire or other metal. An **insulator** is a material that does not conduct electricity, such as the plastic casing around wire.

Preparation

Use the wire cutters to cut the holiday light string into small pieces, leaving 1 bulb between several inches of wire. Use the wire strippers to strip a 1-inch segment of the plastic insulation off either end of each holiday light segment.

A. Give each team a working flashlight and a copy of Attachment 7. Instruct students to follow the directions on Attachment 7.

B. Share the Background Information, then ask students the following questions:
- What components of a flashlight make it work? (bulb, battery, casing)
- What do you think happens when you touch the bulb directly to the battery? (nothing, because the circuit was not completed)

C. Explain that the path electricity flows through is called a circuit. A circuit must be complete for the bulb to light. Ask students what a light switch does when it is flipped to the on position. (It completes the circuit.)

D. Complete the following circuit experiment:
- Sit with students in a circle with hands on their knees, palms up.
- Have each student place his or her left hand on top of the right hand of the person to his or her left.
- Start the "flow" of electricity by tapping the hand of the person to your right with your left hand. Have students continue until the circuit is completed once around the circle.
- Start the circuit again and quickly scoot out of the circle. Have students discuss analogies that can be made between this game and flipping a light switch on and off. Example: complete: incomplete :: light : dark.

E. Have students build circuits using Attachment 8. After they build their circuits, have them test items for conductivity. Have students create a T-chart in their journals showing items that are conductors and items that are insulators.

Conductors	Insulators
paper clip	cotton ball
penny	plastic ruler

F. Invite students to research scientists who helped in the process of building a flashlight. Students may use the following Web sites to help in their research. As always, please preview the sites before allowing student access.

- **http://www.thomasedison.com/biog.htm**
- **http://sln.fi.edu/franklin/scientst/scientst.html**
- **http://library.thinkquest.org/C004471/tep/en/biographies/benjamin_franklin.html?tqskip1=1&tqtime=0404**

G. Ask students to produce a report about how the contributions of Benjamin Franklin and Thomas Edison led to the development of the flashlight. Remind students that you will use the rubrics on Attachments 1 and 2 to evaluate their reports and presentations. Then have students research the history of the flashlight using the following Web sites:

> **Teacher Tip**
> **SCAMPER** can be used to help students develop new thoughts and ideas and aids the creative thinking process. SCAMPER is an acronym for: **s**ubstitute, **c**ombine, **a**dapt, **m**odify/**m**agnify/**m**inify, **p**ut to other uses, **e**liminate, **r**everse/rearrange.

- **http://www.geocities.com/~stuarts1031/flashlight.html**
- **http://inventors.about.com/library/inventors/blflashlight.htm**

H. Tell students to be creative in their presentation styles. Here are some ideas:
- Write a "This is Your Life" game show script with the flashlight as the guest.
- Imagine you are the flashlight and write an autobiography.
- Produce an interview tape of Benjamin Franklin and Thomas Edison telling how they contributed to the development of the flashlight.

I. Have students write a 5-10 question quiz that can be taken after listening to their reports. Students may wish to build a circuit board, writing the questions on one side and the answers on the other. When the circuit they created earlier is touched to the correct question and answer, the bulb lights. Encourage students to work with cardboard, insulated wire, duct tape, and their circuits to develop the quiz boards.

J. Invite students to present their reports and quiz boards to the class.

Closure

A. Have students write in their journals about the contributions of Thomas Edison and Benjamin Franklin. Ask students to imagine what life would be like without electricity.

B. Ask students to write two generalizations about how electricity affects our lives. Here are some examples to get them started:
- Electricity has positive and negative effects on our lives.
- Without electricity, many things would not be possible.

Extensions

A. Encourage students to use the components of a circuit to create an innovation that could help people. Encourage students to keep a detailed process record as they work through the following steps:

- Research to see that no similar products exist.
- Draw a model of the innovation, then build a model. It does not have to work. The idea is the most important thing.
- Write a report telling how this innovation will have a positive impact on many lives.

B. Have students set up displays with their products. Invite other classes to listen to presentations. Construct a bar graph with all innovations listed and allow students from other classes to tally the innovation they believe would be most helpful.

Assessment

A. Assess reports, quiz boards, and presentations using Attachments 1 and 2.

B. Use Attachment 3 to assess generalizations

C. Look for ingenuity and a solid process record to assess the Extension activity. If your district or region offers a science fair, encourage students to refine their innovations, check the guidelines for entry, and enter their projects in the science fair.

Notes

Activity 5 — Explore Systems in Your State

Differentiation Strategies

Analysis and Synthesis
- Drawing Conclusions
- Evaluate Situations

Multiple Perspectives
- Inquiry
- Shared Inquiry

Methodology and Use of Resources
- Note Taking
- Research

Enduring Understanding
Systems may provide a way to organize and categorize things.

Guiding Question
(C) Why does each state have unique characteristics?

Instructional Materials
- books about your state
- journals
- computer with Internet access

Background Information
Each state has **characteristics** that make it different, including geographic **landforms**, historic sites, modern transportation systems, and innovative school systems.

Preparation
Gather books from the library about your state. Be sure the resources include geographical features, regional information, and information about your state.

A. Begin a discussion about what makes your state unique. Have students brainstorm physical, economic, historic, and **regional** characteristics.

B. Invite students to discuss how the items in the brainstormed list are part of a system in the state. For example, if you lived in Texas and cited Fort Davis as a historical feature, you could say Fort Davis was once part of the state's defense system.

C. Have pairs of students select one system statement from the previous step to explore and research. Have them develop a written report and visuals to present to the class. Remind students that the rubrics on Attachments 1 and 2 will be used to evaluate their reports and presentations. Have students include the following in their reports:
- a graph showing statistical information about the system they selected to research
- some historical background about the system
- geographic features near the system

- how the system contributes to the economy of the state (if applicable)
- how the system will help the state in the future (if applicable)

D. Allow students to choose other ways to present their information besides written reports. Encourage students to be creative.

E. Invite students to present their work to the class. Encourage the class to take notes in their journals about the presentations.

Closure

A. Have students share the notes they took during presentations. Have students answer the following questions in their journals:
- What was the most interesting thing you learned about your state?
- What was the most interesting thing you uncovered as you researched?

B. Have students write two generalizations in their journals about systems in their state. Here are two examples to get them started:
- Texas' transportation system has a wide variety of structures that make it unique.
- The geographical features of Louisiana cause many of the roads to be raised.

Extensions

A. Encourage students to select another state to research. Have them research the same issues they researched for their own state.

B. Have students compare and contrast the issues between the states and present their information to the class. Ask the class to take notes on the new presentations and compare the data. Have them write about which state is better to live in and why.

C. Invite students to share their opinions with the class.

Assessment

A. Use Attachments 1 and 2 to evaluate the reports and presentations.

B. You may choose to use the blank rubric on Attachment 4 to develop a new assessment tool if students are working on projects other than written reports with visuals. Enlist the help of students to create the new assessment tool before they begin work on the project. Students should know how they will be assessed before beginning their projects.

Differentiation Strategies
Analysis and Synthesis
- Generalizations
- Drawing Conclusions
- Evaluation

Instructional Materials
- string
- several sets of Cuisenaire Rods or the centimeter cubes and rods torn from the back of a consumable math book
- rulers
- journals

Enduring Understanding
Systems may provide a common denominator for people to understand many topics

Guiding Questions
(F) What is the metric system?
(P) Should every country in the world use the metric system?

Background Information
Students need experience using the **metric** system. Most countries use the metric system as their standard form of measurement. All scientists use the metric system.

The metric system has three standard words for measuring length, weight (mass), and capacity (volume): meters, grams, and liters. The metric system adds **prefixes** to these root words to convey meaning. The prefixes with their meanings are listed for you:

milli — one-thousandth   deca — ten
centi — one-hundredth   hecto — hundred
deci — one-tenth   kilo — thousand

You can set these prefixes up on a number line with the root word measurement in the middle like the example below:

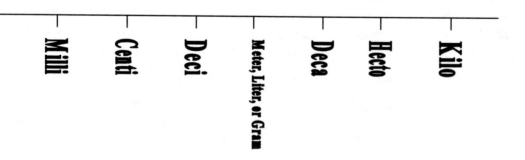

A. Distribute a set of manipulatives to pairs of students. Ask students to work with the centimeter and decimeter blocks. Have them determine the number of centimeter blocks that make the length of one decimeter block. (10) Tell students that 10 centimeters equal one decimeter.

B. Draw the chart (from the previous page) on the chalkboard. Ask students to identify the name of the measurement system that uses these prefixes. Ask students to hypothesize what the prefix *milli* means. (thousand) Explain that 1 millimeter is one/thousandth of a meter.(There are 1,000 millimeters in a meter) Tell students that a meter is about as long as a yard stick. Show students the millimeters marked on a standard 12-inch ruler. Ask students to determine the number of millimeters on one 12-inch ruler. (approximately 305)

C. Show students where centimeters are on their rulers. Then ask the following questions:
- How many centimeters do you think there are in a meter? (100)
- How many millimeters are there in a centimeter? (10)
- What does the prefix *centi-* mean? (one hundredth)

D. Tell students that a decimeter is one-tenth of a meter. Ask students how many decimeters equal a meter. (10) Then ask the following questions:
- How many centimeters are in a decimeter? (10)
- How many millimeters are in a decimeter? (100)
- What does the prefix *deci-* mean? (one-tenth)

E. Invite students to use their rulers to find an item in the room that measures about a millimeter (about the thickness of a credit card), one item that measures about a centimeter (pencil eraser), one item that measures about a decimeter (a new crayon), and one item that measures about a meter (the width of the doorway).

F. Have students create a chart in their journals like the one below.

Body part	Estimate	Actual	Difference
length across eye			
length of ear			
length of nose			
length of head			
length of thigh			
height			

Be sure students choose the appropriate unit of measurement then measure each part listed above.

G. Have students determine what fractional part of their height their head contributes. (about 1/3 of the height of children is attributed to the head)

H. Have students discuss metric measurements provided on food and drink items such as soda cans and packages of cookies. Ask students why they think these measurements are provided in addition to more familiar measurements such as ounces.

I. Tell students that a paper clip weighs about a gram. Ask students to use grams and determine the prefix they would add to measure their own weight. (kilograms) Have students estimate their weight in kilograms. If scales are available, have students weigh themselves. If the measurement is in pounds, use the following formula to convert the weight to kilograms: # of pounds x 0.454 = weight in kilograms

Example: 63 pounds x 0.454 = 28.6 kilograms

J. Have students estimate then calculate about how many paper clips they weigh. In the example above:
The student weighs 28.6 kilograms, or 28,600 grams. So the student weighs about as much as 28,600 paper clips.

Closure
A. Ask students to discuss the importance of understanding and using the metric system. Have students list three things in their journals they like about the metric system.

B. Have students write two generalizations about the metric system. Here are two examples to get them started:
- There are pros and cons about using the metric system.
- The metric system influences the teaching of math and the study of science.

Extensions
A. Have students debate the pros and cons of converting the United States to the metric system in one day. Have one team support America making the switch in a day. The other team should oppose that point.

B. Have teams brainstorm pros and cons to converting all measurement to the metric system then hold the debate. Then have students decide the best form of measurement for the United States.

C. Have students write a story about how it would feel to be one centimeter tall. The story could be from the viewpoint of a beetle, a blade of grass, or any other small object. Encourage students to illustrate the story using an "ant's eye" point of view. Have students read their stories and share their illustrations with the class.

Assessment
A. Assess student estimations and measurements to be sure they chose the most appropriate units in which to measure.

B. Assess the stories using Attachment 1.

Activity 7 — A Single Shard

Differentiation Strategies

Innovation and Application
- Flexibility
- Extend Boundaries

Analysis and Synthesis
- Generalizations
- Aesthetic Thinking

Communication
- Research
- Writing Skills

Relevance and Significance
- Field Lesson
- Resource Person

Enduring Understanding

Systems may provide a common denominator for people to understand many topics.

Guiding Questions

(F) What is meant by learning a trade?
(C) Why is passing down a trade a cultural tradition in Korea?

Instructional Materials
- multiple matching copies of *A Single Shard* book, by Linda Sue Park
- journals

Background Information

A Single Shard, the 2001 Newbery Medal winner, is about an orphan living in 12th-century Korea. All men in the story pass down their **trades** to their sons, but because he has no father, the boy has no one to teach him a trade. The boy, Tree-Ear, becomes fascinated with a potter who crafts **celadon** pottery. As he watches and then works for the potter, Tree-Ear learns many valuable lessons about life.

A. Have small teams read the Acknowledgements and first two chapters, then ask students to discuss the following questions:
- Why is it funny when Crane-man asks, "Have you hungered well today?"
- Do you think going through garbage is more honorable than begging? Explain.
- What did Crane-man mean with the following statement? "Scholars read the great words of the world. But you and I must learn to read the world itself."
- How did Tree-Ear get his name?
- What system did Tree-Ear and Crane-man work out to obtain food and keep their home clean?
- How do you think Min designed the rectangle box? What system did he use?

B. Invite students to read aloud chapters 3 and 4 as a class, then ask teams to create questions about the chapters. Encourage the class to create a game using the questions. The game could be a trivia game, a Jeopardy!-like game, etc. Ask students to write rules for the game, then allow them to play the games.

C. Have students read chapters 5-7 on their own and answer the following questions in their journals:

- Describe how you would feel if you were in Tree-Ear's shoes. Min basically ignores or shouts at Tree-Ear. Tree-Ear does all the chores Min doesn't want to do anymore: cutting wood, getting clay, draining the clay. How might these chores be helpful to Tree-Ear someday?
- Tree-Ear hopes that he will someday sit at the potter's wheel. Would you be this patient waiting for your turn? Write a short essay about something you have waited or are waiting patiently to do. How are your desires alike and different from Tree-Ear's?
- The concept of stealing another's ideas and making them your own is called plagiarism. Writers, artists, musicians, and others are protected by law against plagiarism by use of copyrights and trademarks. How did Kang protect his work? How did Tree-Ear honor this protection? What would you have done in this situation?
- Describe Tree-Ear's "ah-ha" moment, when he was draining the white clay. Describe a time when you had a sudden understanding about something.

D. Assign four small teams and have each read either chapter 8, 9, 10, or 11. Then challenge each team to write a script and perform a short play to tell what happened. Have students perform their plays in order of the chapters.

E. Have students read chapters 12-13 as a class. Have them discuss whether *A Single Shard* is a good title for the book.

Closure

Have students write several generalizations about the book. Here are two examples to get them started:

- The tools, techniques, and innovations of celadon pottery-making led Min to get the commission.
- Life for an orphan was difficult in the 12th century.

Extensions

A. Have students choose a different method of reporting about a book. They should create the report then make a small clay pot to accompany the report. You may want to enlist the help of an art teacher. They may also want to create questions and responses using the Six Hat Thinking by Dr. de Bono.

B. Encourage students to research celadon

Teacher Tip
Six Thinking Hats-created by Dr. de Bono in the 1980s.
White Hat – Facts
Red Hat – Feeling and emotions
Black Hat – Judgment and caution
Yellow Hat – Logical Positive
Green Hat – Creativity
Blue Hat – Process Control

C. Ask the art teacher at your school about scheduling a pottery wheel demonstration or about obtaining clay for your students to mold into items from the story.

Assessment
Assess student writing using Attachment 1. You may use the blank rubric on Attachment 4 to create an assessment tool to assess the plays and the game created by students.

Notes

_____

_____

_____

_____

_____

_____

_____

_____

_____

_____

_____

_____

_____

_____

_____

_____

Activity 8 — Culture of Transportation

Differentiation Strategies

Analysis and Synthesis
- Evaluate Situations
- Draw Conclusions

Multiple Perspectives
- Point of View
- Shared Inquiry

Communication
- Creative Writing
- Research

Enduring Understanding
Systems may improve the quality of life for some people.

Guiding Questions
(F) How has the railroad changed our culture?
(C) Why do some people feel that western expansion was detrimental?

Instructional Materials
- several social studies textbooks focusing on your state's history
- computer with Internet access
- journals

Background Information
American history was greatly influenced by the development of the steam engine. The steam engine led to the development of the **locomotive**. Powered by burning wood or coal, the train could travel great distances in less time than the traditional horse and wagon. After the development of the train, track builders could not lay track fast enough. Many men left their families to help build the tracks that crossed America. When they found an area they wanted to settle, they sent for their families to come. Trains became the bridge across America and helped shape the **structure** of the United States.

The development of the locomotive greatly changed the faces of American and Native-American cultures. It also had **detrimental** effects on wildlife, such as the American bison. In this activity, students search for evidence showing how the beginnings of the transportation system changed cultures forever.

A. Share the Background Information. Lead students in a discussion about the influences the railroad had on American and Native-American cultures.

B. Ask students to research the changes the railroad had on our culture from different viewpoints. Have students consider one of the following viewpoints:
- a man working as a track layer away from his family
- a woman raising children in the city by herself
- a tribe of Native-Americans relocated for the passage of the train

- a massive herd of bison
- a town of people in California

C. Have pairs of students choose one of the topics above to research. They will need to go beyond the textbook. Here are two Web sites that may be helpful. As always, please preview all sites before allowing students to view them.
- **http://www.nps.gov/jeff/LewisClark2/HomePage/HomePage.htm**
- **http://www.pbs.org/ktca/farmhouses/**

D. Visit the following Web site that contains the words to a Schoolhouse Rock song about expansion.
- **http://www.apocalypse.org/pub/u/gilly/Schoolhouse_Rock/HTML/history/elbow.html**

E. Have students share their findings with the class. Encourage the class to put together a magazine article in the format of National Geographic. The article should weave all information gathered to tell about the railroad's effects on the culture then and now.

F. Have students print out their articles on the computer. Encourage them to find pictures or create illustrations to go with their articles.

Closure
A. Have students write several generalizations about westward expansion and its effects on different cultures at the time. Here are two generalizations to get them started:
- The transcontinental railroad greatly influenced the cultures of the time.
- Westward expansion had positive and negative consequences.

B. Have students discuss their feelings about westward expansion. Use the following guiding questions: Was it inevitable? Was it necessary? Was it necessary to remove Native-Americans from their homes? What positives came from westward expansion? What negatives came from westward expansion?

Extensions
A. Have students write about what might have happened if the railroad had never been completed. Ask them: How might our history be different? How might our culture be different today?

B. Have students research other animals that were hunted to the brink of extinction because of westward expansion.

Assessment
Use Attachment 1 to assess student articles. You may wish to create a new rubric to assess the discussion in the Extension activity. Student responses should show a depth of understanding beyond the ordinary.

Activity 9 — When Do You Party?

Differentiation Strategies
Knowledge and Skills
- Draw Conclusions
- Inquiry
- Observation

Communication
- Demonstration
- Research

Relevance and Significance
- Resource Person
- Group Consensus

Enduring Understanding
Systems may provide a way to organize and categorize things.

Guiding Questions
(F) What aspects of a culture can be found in traditional celebrations?
(C) Why do people strive to maintain traditional celebrations?

Instructional Materials
- computer with Internet access
- books about customs and celebrations in your state

Background Information
Every state has **traditional** celebrations and customs. From Mardi Gras in Louisiana to the Great Wisconsin Cheese Festival, celebrations **preserve** memories all over our country.

Preparation
Create and research a list of annual celebrations in your state. You can get this information from your state's department of tourism.

A. Have students brainstorm annual celebrations in your community. Here are some examples: Independence Day, Memorial Day, May Fest, and Spring Fest.

B. Share the customs and celebrations you researched earlier. (See Preparation.)

C. Encourage pairs of students to select one or two of the celebrations or customs in your state to research. Help them research the following:

- What is the origin of the celebration?
- What are the events during the celebration?
- Who is in charge of planning and implementing the celebration?
- Are **customary** foods served at the celebration? If so, which ones?
- Who usually attends the celebration?
- When is it held? How often?
- Where does the celebration occur?
- If the celebration occurs away from your city, have students consult a state map to plan simple driving directions to get to the celebration.

D. Have students put the information about the celebration into a brochure format. The brochure should be written as an advertisement persuading people to participate. Enlist the help of students to create a new rubric using Attachment 4 to assess the brochures.

E. Invite students to present their brochures to the class. Display the brochures on a table or bulletin board.

Closure
Ask students to write to the following prompt in their journals:
What is the most significant part of keeping customs and traditions alive?

Extension
Have students contact a person in charge of planning a celebration they researched in their city. Encourage students to ask the person to set up a brochure contest as a part of their celebration this year. The contest could be open to fourth-grade students. Volunteer to help get the word out about the contest. Have students find businesspeople to act as judges. Find a place to display the winning brochures during the celebration.

Assessment
Use the rubric created by the students to assess the brochures.

Notes

_____

_____

_____

_____

_____

_____

Activity 10 — Did You Hear the One About...

Differentiation Strategies
Knowledge and Skills
- Inquiry
- Inferences

Analysis and Synthesis
- Generalizations
- Evaluation Situations

Methodology and Use of Resources
- Note Taking
- Resource Person
- Research

Instructional Materials
- journals
- computers

Enduring Understanding
Systems may improve the quality of life for some people.

Guiding Questions
(F) What family stories are passed down from generation to generation in your family?
(F) What is the drawback to only using an oral history to remember family stories?

Background Information
People from past cultures, especially **ancient** cultures, had a system of passing along stories and traditions for their children to carry on. These lessons, events, and celebrations were told as stories. By passing stories from one **generation** to the next, ancestors made sure people would remember what happened in the past, helping them make good decisions in the future.

There is much literature devoted to the retelling of stories from the past. **Myths** and **legends** derive from stories told to teach lessons and to help explain the world around us.

This activity allows students to learn stories from their past and to write them down so they will be able to share the stories with their grandchildren.

Preparation
Think of a story told to you about an event in your family. The story should be old enough that you are not a part of it. Practice telling the story with dramatic expression. Make the story interesting to see and hear.

A. Share the Background Information.

B. Provide background about your family and the story you will tell. Tell your story. If you thought of more than one story, tell more.

C. Tell students that people of past generations depended heavily on the oral tradition of storytelling to pass on the family history. Explain that students will now have the opportunity to compile a book of stories from their family history.

D. Have students brainstorm a list of people they would like to interview to find their stories. Good sources might include grandparents, parents, aunts, and uncles.

E. Encourage students to write, e-mail, or call relatives and take notes about the stories. Have students ask about photographs or illustrations of the people or events in the stories.

F. Have students write family stories on the computer. Encourage students to go through the peer-editing process. Use the blank rubric on Attachment 4 to create a new assessment for the books students will write. Enlist the help of students in determining the criteria for evaluation.

G. Have students scan photographs or illustrations into their text. You may need to enlist the help of a technology specialist at your campus.

H. Instruct students to create a cover, table of contents, and a dedication page for their books and insert these into the document on the computer.

I. Invite students to share stories from their completed books with the class.

Closure
Have students reflect about their projects in their journals. Have them answer the following questions:
- What was the most interesting thing you learned about your family?
- Who in your family was most instrumental in helping you write your book?
- What stories do you hope to pass on to your children and grandchildren?

Extensions
A. Have students think of two significant stories in their lives that they wish to pass along to their children and grandchildren. Encourage students to write the stories and include photographs or illustrations with the text. Have them add the stories to their books.

B. Have students invite the people who helped tell the family stories in their books to a "Reading Restaurant." Serve refreshments and have students create "menus" with the titles of their stories on them. Friends and relatives will enjoy listening to students read about their family histories.

Assessment
Use the rubric created by the students to assess the books written by students.

Activity 11 — Why Do Raindrops Keep Falling on My Head?

Differentiation Strategies

Analysis and Synthesis
- Generalizations
- Evaluation

Multiple Perspectives
- Shared Inquiry
- Evaluate Situations

Communication
- Demonstration
- Uses Technological Media

Instructional Materials
- several bowls
- water
- clear jar with a lid
- ice cubes

Optional:
- hot plate
- small pan with water

Background Information

Every day when the sun comes out it heats the surface of the Earth, beginning a process called **evaporation**. Puddles, lakes, oceans, even the dew on plants, evaporate. Evaporation is the process of a liquid changing into a gas. When heated by the sun, water breaks down into tiny **molecules** that float into the air. We call this gas **water vapor**. The water vapor rises to the cooler air above. As it cools, the water vapor collects together around other particles floating in the air. These particles can be

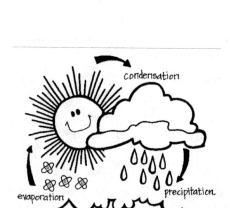

specs of dust, salt, or even small bugs. This collection of water molecules forms a cloud in a process called **condensation**. As the water vapor continues to condense, the cloud gets larger and heavier. The water vapor molecules bond together until they are too heavy to remain in the cloud and fall back to the ground in the form of rain. This is called **precipitation**. The precipitation falls and the last stage in the water cycle, **accumulation**, occurs. Then the cycle begins again. The water cycle is a system we depend on every day. Without the water cycle, Earth would dry up and become a vast desert.

Preparation

Prepare ice cubes before class. Fill two bowls 2/3 full of water. Mark the level of the water in each bowl using a crayon. Place both bowls in direct sunlight, one inside the school and one outside. Leave both bowls for several hours before the lesson begins. Retrieve the bowls before class begins.

A. Direct attention to the two bowls. Tell students that the bowls had the same amount of water at the beginning of the day. Draw attention to the crayon lines. Tell students that the water mysteriously disappeared. Have students brainstorm possible ways that the water disappeared. When someone guesses evaporation, move on with the lesson.

B. Tell students you filled up the bowls at the same time and ask them to hypothesize why one bowl contains less water. Students should realize that one bowl was in a hotter area and the water evaporated faster.

C. Ask students what happens to water after it evaporates. (It condenses into clouds in the atmosphere) Share the Background Information, then ask students to hypothesize what makes water vapor condense. (As it rises into the atmosphere it cools, causing it to condense into liquid form again.)

D. Share the following dialogue: Most of our rainwater comes from the oceans. What is the ocean nearest you called? Imagine that every year 79 inches of that ocean evaporated. How tall is that? (Remind students to divide 79 by 12 to find height in feet. Ask for a volunteer to go to the chalkboard and demonstrate how to divide the two numbers. (The answer is 6, remainder 7, or 6-feet-7 inches.) Have students use a ruler or yardstick and masking tape to mark the height on the wall of your classroom.

E. Share the following with students: Have you ever swam in the deep end of a pool? Some deep ends are 6 feet or deeper. This can give you an idea of the amount that evaporates from the surface of the oceans. Have students predict whether oceans lose water. (They do.) Ask students to share how the water returns to the oceans. (through rain at sea and runoff produced by rainstorms on land)

F. Ask for volunteers to perform the experiment on Attachment 9.

G. In their journals, have students answer the following questions:
- How does the Water Cycle in a Jar experiment relate to the water cycle?
- How does the Water Cycle in a Jar experiment relate to weather?
- Where else have you ever noticed condensation?
- What conclusions can you draw about the water cycle from the experiment?
- How does the ocean affect the weather on Earth?

H. Have students predict what would happen if one part of the water cycle suddenly disappeared. Ask them: What would happen to the water cycle if the sun did not shine? What would happen to the water cycle and Earth if the water vapor escaped out of Earth's atmosphere and into space?

Closure

A. Have students write several generalizations about weather and the water cycle. Here are two generalizations to get them started:
- Evaporation requires water and the sun.
- The water cycle and weather patterns are related.

B. Invite students to share generalizations with the class. Ask students to discuss how the water cycle is a system. Ask them how the system changes from day to day and from area to area.

Extensions

A. Have students research the characteristics of Earth's atmosphere that allow the water cycle to occur. Invite them to develop an informative documentary with visuals or a PowerPoint presentation explaining the differences between Earth's atmosphere and the atmospheres (or lack of atmospheres) surrounding other planets. Have students create a special rubric for evaluating their documentaries and visuals. Invite students to self-assess after presenting the documentaries. Assess the documentaries yourself, then meet with each student or team to discuss your evaluations.

B. Challenge students to develop a way to demonstrate the movement of water through the water cycle. One idea might be to evaporate water dyed blue to a lid colored in dried red food coloring, resulting in purple "precipitation." They may also want to illustrate the water cycle using the Pyramid pattern on Attachment 13.

Assessment

A. Assess student journal responses for reasonableness. Be sure students can verbalize the water cycle process and understand the effects of removing one part of the cycle.

B. Assess generalizations using Attachment 3.

Notes

_____

_____

_____

_____

_____

_____

_____

_____

Activity 12 — We Are Not the Weakest Link

Differentiation Strategies
Knowledge and Skills
- Sequencing
- Inquiry

Analysis and Synthesis
- Drawing Conclusions
- Generalizations
- Critical Thinking

Communication
- Research
- Uses Technological Media

Enduring Understanding
Systems may provide a common denominator for people to understand many topics.

Guiding Questions
(F) What are the roles of the producers, consumers and decomposers in a food chain?

(C) How does the loss of a member in a food chain impact the entire food chain?

Instructional Materials
- books from the library about food chains and food webs
- journals
- computer with Internet access

Background Information
The sun is the major source of energy for the Earth. Without the sun, we would probably perish. From the amoeba to the blue whale, we all depend on the sun for survival.

The sun is the focal point of our solar system. All nine planets, their moons, asteroids, comets, etc., orbit the sun. The heat energy from the sun helps keep our planet warm. It also provides energy for plants to grow.

Plants produce their own food in a process called **photosynthesis**. All animals, whether **herbivores** (plant eaters), **carnivores** (meat eaters), or **omnivores** (meat and plant eaters) depend on plants for survival. At some point in the food chain, everything leads back to the plants and sun.

Preparation
Write the following sets of words on the chalkboard:

rabbit	lettuce	fox		
person	milk	cow	grass	
leaf	sparrow	worm	hawk	
killer whale	plankton	seal	salmon	shrimp

Obtain permission from your principal for your students to create a class Web site about ecology. Enlist the help of a technology specialist at your school to help.

A. Invite students to study each group of words. Ask students to determine the kind of system to which these groups of words belong. (food chains)

B. Distribute journals and ask students to place the things in each list in order from the top to the bottom of the food chain (i.e., killer whale, seal, salmon, shrimp, plankton). Ask students to write to the following prompt in their journals:
How are food chains systems?

C. Have students share the completed food chains and their responses from their journals. Ask students what they think is the most important part of the food chain. Allow students to discuss for several minutes.

D. Allow students to view the movie about food chains at the following Web site. As always, please preview all sites before allowing students to access them.
http://magma.nationalgeographic.com/ngexplorer/0309/quickflicks/

E. Allow students to visit the following sites to learn more about producers, consumers, and decomposers.
http://www.kidskonnect.com/FoodChain/FoodChainHome.html
http://www.eagle.ca/~matink/themes/Biomes/foodweb.html

F. Have students consider removing one element of a given food web by playing the following game:
- Assign one student to be the sun and to sit in the center of a circle. Have all other students form a circle around the sun.
- Assign students to play the following parts:

Producers — plants and other organisms that produce their own food
Primary consumers — organisms that eat only producers
Secondary consumers — organisms that eat primary consumers and/or producers
Decomposers — organisms that help break down deceased producers and consumers

- Ask students to arrange themselves into food chains. Each food chain should begin with a producer, and contain one primary and one secondary consumer. Each food chain should sit side-by-side in the circle.
- Go around the circle and choose one person from each team to leave the ecosystem.
- Have students discuss the ramifications of losing that part of the chain.
- Invite remaining students to regroup to form new food chains.
- Go around the circle again and select one person randomly from each team to leave the ecosystem. Have students discuss the ramifications of the loss.
- Ask the sun to leave the circle. Have students discuss the short-term and long-term effects of the sun being gone from the ecosystem.

G. Invite students to create a game that teaches about food chains for younger students. They should develop a simple set of directions and rules for the game, which should teach the following information:
- what a food chain is
- producers, consumers, and decomposers
- the consequences of losing any part of the food chain
- the importance of the sun in every food chain

H. Have students teach their games and play them with a second- or third-grade class.

Closure

A. Tell students that when we generalize, we consider many things we have learned and make a single statement about them. Provide the following examples:
- The field of mathematics deals with numbers.
- There are many kinds of pasta.
- The study of Earth and outer space are interrelated.
- Disease can be both a cause and effect.

B. Have students brainstorm generalizations that can be made about school to practice. For example:
- Summer vacation has positive and negative consequences.
- Junk food machines in schools lead to poor nutrition and obesity in children.

C. Ask students to write in their journals two generalizations about the sun and food chains. Here are some examples to get them started:
- The sun is the most important part of the food chain.
- Removing even one part of a food chain affects the larger food web.

D. Invite students to share their generalizations with the class. Go over the rubric on Attachment 3, explaining that generalizations will be evaluated using that rubric.

Extensions

A. Invite students to use the following questions or create their own to research:
- How do harmful pesticides disrupt the food chain?
- What might happen if all the coyotes in an ecosystem suddenly disappeared?

B. Have students research a question and present their research in a report. Have students produce a visual (such as an illustrated food web) to go along with the reports. Encourage students to have a friend peer edit their work. Share the writing rubric on Attachment 1. Explain that you will use that rubric to evaluate their writing. Share the presentation rubric as well. Use the presentation rubric to evaluate student presentations.

C. Have students present their reports to the class. Display student reports and visuals created on a bulletin board.

D. Encourage students to create a class Web site about ecosystems. You can enlist the help of the technology specialist at your school to help. Have students take digital photos of their visuals and post their reports to the site. As students work further in their studies of systems and ecology, have them add their new information to the site.

Assessment
Assess student generalizations from the Closure activity using Attachment 3.

Notes

_____

_____

_____

_____

_____

_____

_____

_____

_____

_____

_____

_____

_____

_____

_____

_____

_____

Activity 13 — Weather or Not

Differentiation Strategies

Knowledge and Skills
- Attributes
- Categorizing
- Observation

Analysis and Synthesis
- Generalizations
- Drawing Conclusions

Methodology and Use of Resources
- Resource Person
- Research

Instructional Materials
- computer with Internet access
- books about weather

Background Information

Earth's climate is supported by the sun, the warmth from inside Earth's core, the Arctic temperatures at the poles, wind currents, and the oceans. For life to exist as we know it, all these characteristics must work together in a giant system.

The weather is affected by all of the factors mentioned above. **Weather** is defined as the state of the **atmosphere** in relation to temperature, pressure, humidity, wind, and cloudiness. A weather system is an area showing a marked change in the state of the atmosphere in relation to temperature, pressure, humidity, wind, and cloudiness.

A. Ask students to discuss how weather is a system. Share the Background Information.

B. Have students brainstorm kinds of weather. Then allow students to form teams to research weather systems. They may use the books you collected earlier and the Web sites below. Please preview all sites before allowing student access.
http://teacher.scholastic.com/activities/wwatch/winter/index.htm
http://kids.mtpe.hq.nasa.gov/archive/nino/index.html

© Prufrock Press Inc.

http://www.eagle.ca/~matink/themes/Biomes/foodweb.html
http://www.ucar.edu/educ_outreach/webweather/

C. Have students create a profile of the weather for each season in your region. Ask them to list the most common forecasts during the four seasons.

D. Have students research other data about your region, including average rainfall per month and per year, average temperature, average humidity, etc. Have students relate the monthly averages to the weather systems that affect your region.

E. Invite students to create a pamphlet about your region. Create a new rubric to evaluate pamphlets using Attachment 4. The pamphlets should be directed toward people considering moving to your community and include the following information:
- general information about your city such as population, elevation, and size
- local attractions such as amusement parks or sports parks
- general school information
- an overview of seasonal weather
- illustrations or scanned photos of interesting places in your city

F. Invite students to present their pamphlets to the class. Have the class choose the most inviting pamphlet.

Closure
A. Have students write to the following prompt in their journals:
How do you think climate and weather systems affect the populations of towns in the United States? What kind of weather would you avoid if you were considering moving to another region of the country?

B. Instruct students to write two generalizations about weather systems in their journals. Here are two examples to get them started:
- Weather systems can be both a cause and an effect.
- Weather systems are not man-made, but can be affected by things we do to the Earth.

Extension
Invite a meteorologist to speak. Have students prepare by reviewing interview etiquette and generating questions to ask. Have students share their pamphlets with your guest.

Assessment
Evaluate the pamphlets using the rubric created by the students. Evaluate generalizations using Attachment 3. Check student process records for information they found regarding weather systems. Remind students to take notes often.

Activity 14 — Adaptations in Systems

Differentiation Strategies
Knowledge and Skills
- Attributes
- Demonstration

Analysis and Synthesis
- Generalizations
- Drawing Conclusions
- Evaluate Situations

Instructional Materials
- computer with Internet access
- books about different ecosystems, plants, and animals

> ### Enduring Understanding
> Systems may provide a way to organize and categorize things.
>
> ### Guiding Questions
> (F) What is an ecosystem?
> (F) What is adaptation?
> (C) If an ecosystem changes, what determines if an organism survives?

A. Ask students to define the word *ecosystem*. (the interaction of living things with their environment)

B. Have students brainstorm several ecosystems. Possible responses include lakes, forests, ocean, sandbox, backyard, desert, and polar regions.

C. Discuss how some animals adapt to live safely in their ecosystems. Help students visit the following Web site to research the lives of snowshoe hares. As always, please preview the site before allowing student access:
http://www.cws-scf.ec.gc.ca/hww-fap/hww-fap.cfm?ID_species=73&lang=e

D. Encourage students to brainstorm other animals that **adapt** to their changing environment, including the white-tailed deer, arctic foxes, black bears, and skunks.

E. Have each student select an animal to research. Each student should keep a process record of notes listing the following information:
- What animal is being researched? Where is this animal's natural **habitat**? Draw a map to show where this animal lives.
- In what ecosystem does this animal exist?
- What are some unique characteristics of this animal?
- What adaptations must this animal make to survive?
- What does this animal eat? Is this animal a predator or prey?
- Construct a food chain that includes this animal.
- What is the life span of this animal? Create a graph that shows the life span compared to other animals in the same ecosystem.

- How often does this animal reproduce? Create a table showing the number of offspring produced by a single animal.
- Make predictions about what might happen if this animal suddenly disappeared from its ecosystem. How would the ecosystem be affected? Would our lives be impacted in some way if the animal became extinct?

F. Have students arrange the information in their process records into an informative oral report or publish the report and make a book. The visuals should be used as a part of the presentation. Tell students you will use the rubrics on Attachments 1 and 2 for assessment purposes.

G. Invite students to share their reports with the class.

Closure
Ask students to write to the following prompt in their journals:
Are ecosystems fragile? Explain your answer by citing specific information from the reports you heard earlier.

Extensions
A. Encourage students to extend their projects by building model ecosystems. Create a new rubric using Attachment 4 to assess this assignment. Enlist the help of students to create the rubric before they begin constructing their models.

B. Have students display their reports or books, models, and visuals on tables in the library or in a hallway. Have students share their reports with other classes.

Assessment
Use Attachments 1 and 2 to assess reports and presentations.

Notes

_____

_____

_____

_____

_____

_____

_____

_____

_____

Activity 15 — The Disappearance of Systems Past

Differentiation Strategies

Analysis and Synthesis
- Drawing Conclusions
- Problem Defining

Ethics/Unanswered Questions
- Provocative Questions
- Evaluate Situations

Multiple Perspectives
- Shared Inquiry
- Group Consensus

Enduring Understanding
The word systems, has many meanings.

Guiding Questions
(F) What factors may have contributed to the mass extinction of the dinosaurs?
(C) Why should we care how the dinosaurs became extinct?

Instructional Materials
- copies of Attachments 10 and 11 (as needed)
- books and references about dinosaurs and their extinction
- computer with Internet access
- journals

Background Information
One of the greatest **mass extinction** puzzles is the disappearance of the dinosaurs. We have only known of the existence of dinosaurs a very short time, and many theories have risen as to their **demise**.

At one time scientists believed an ice age enveloped Earth, causing plants and animals to die off. But scientists could not explain why the ice age occurred or predict whether it would happen again. In 1980 scientists began to develop the most convincing theory to date about the dinosaur extinction. They discovered a layer of clay they later called the K-T boundary. They found that all dinosaur fossils were uncovered under this layer of clay. Upon further examination, they found high levels of the rare element **iridium** in the clay that suggested a **meteorite** impact with the Earth may have had something to do with the extinction.

Scientists have searched for the possible impact site on Earth's surface for years. Then in the early 1990s, a scientist discovered a possible crater off the coast of Mexico near the Yucatan Peninsula. The size of the crater, the probable size of the meteor, and the speed at which it probably impacted the Earth have left many scientists to conclude that the meteor caused a chain of events that eventually led to the extinction of dinosaurs.

A. Tell students they will use the scientific method to develop a theory. Distribute copies of Attachment 11 to teams of students.

B. Distribute copies of Attachment 10 and ask teams to read the articles. Tell students that these articles represent the observation part of the scientific method. It is now their job to develop a hypothesis about the articles. After they have developed hypotheses, allow students to research the following Web sites to test their predictions and develop theories. As always, please preview all sites before allowing student access:
- **http://web.ukonline.co.uk/a.buckley/dino.htm**
- **http://pubs.usgs.gov/gip/dinosaurs/**
- **http://dinosaurs.eb.com/dinosaurs/grid.html**
- **http://www.ucmp.berkeley.edu/diapsids/extinction.html**

C. Encourage teams to write up their findings and theories in the form of a science journal article. They should cite the process record they kept during their research along with all of the sources they used. Explain to students that the rubric on Attachment 1 will be used to assess this assignment.

D. Have teams present their findings to the class.

Closure
Have students write two generalizations about the dinosaur extinction and two generalizations about the scientific method. Here are two examples to get them started.
- The extinction of dinosaurs was caused by a massive change in climate on Earth.
- The K-T layer of clay was produced by a natural process.

Extensions
A. Have students research other popular theories about the dinosaur extinction. Other theories include:
- The dinosaurs were killed by their allergies.
- The dinosaurs overpopulated and ran out of food.
- The dinosaurs were killed by massive volcanic eruptions all over the Earth.

B. Have students brainstorm other mysteries of science to research. Have them keep a process record and follow the scientific method as they conduct their research. Help students seek out experts in the field to help them with their research.

If students complete the Extension activities, create a new rubric for each project using Attachment 4. Enlist the help of students to create the rubric and be sure they understand the expectations before beginning the project.

Assessment
Assess journal articles using Attachment 1 and generalizations using Attachment 3.

Activity 16 — Post-Assessment

Differentiation Strategies
Knowledge and Skills
- Attributes
- Categorizing

Multiple Perspectives
- Brainstorming

Instructional Materials
- 1 copy of Attachment 5 per student
- journals

Preparation
Cut apart the word cards on Attachment 5 before class begins. Keep the sets of word cards separated. Use a paper clip to hold each set together.

A. Distribute journals and one set of cards to each student.

B. Have students group the cards into three categories and record them in their journals.

C. Challenge students to select one category about which to write. Students should include the following in their reflections:
- How does the category relate to the word systems?
- How are the words in the category interrelated?
- Include several generalizations about systems.

D. Compare the results of the Post-Assessment with the results of the Pre-Assessment. Look for growth in responses and uniqueness in categorizing and reasoning.

Student or Team: _____

Assignment: _____

Directions: Mark the appropriate rating for each criterion. Use these individual ratings to assign an overall rating for the assignment.

RATINGS	0 Working on it!	1 Novice	2 Acceptable	3 Out of the Box!	Not Applicable
Topic	Did not stay on topic	Stayed on topic most of the time	Stayed on topic and demonstrated some elaboration	Stayed on topic with extensive elaboration and application	N/A
Paragraph Structure	None used, one block of text	Details grouped into paragraphs with multiple topics	Details divided between paragraphs focusing on one topic	Well written paragraphs presented in an order that makes sense	N/A
Organization	Not organized	Was somewhat organized	Very organized	Organization far exceeded the standards	N/A
Written Expression	Could not express ideas in written form	Could only express some ideas	Expressed ideas well	Ideas very well expressed and defined; much elaboration	N/A
OVERALL					

Comments:

Attachment 2   Presentation Rubric

Student or Team: _____

Assignment: _____

Directions: Mark the appropriate rating for each criterion. Use these individual ratings to assign an overall rating for the assignment.

RATINGS	0 Working on it!	1 Novice	2 Acceptable	4 Out of the Box!	Not Applicable
Content	Did not stay on topic	Stayed on topic for most of presentation	Stayed on topic and demonstrated some elaboration	Stayed on topic with extensive elaboration and application	N/A
Oral Expression	Could not express ideas	Could only express some ideas	Easy to understand	Very well articulated	N/A
Organization	Not organized	Was somewhat organized	Very organized	Organization far exceeded the standards	N/A
Preparation	Outline incomplete	Outline or preparation doesn't represent entire project	Outline complete, props complete	Outline complete and well-organized, exemplary props	N/A
OVERALL					

Comments:

Attachment 3   Generalization Rubric

Student or Team: _____

Assignment: _____

Directions: Mark the appropriate rating for each criterion. Use these individual ratings to assign an overall rating for the assignment.

RATINGS	0 Working on it!	1 Novice	2 Acceptable	3 Out of the Box!
Generalizations	Unable to make a generalization with help	Begins to make generalizations between ideas with help	Makes simple generalizations with little help	Makes complex generalizations between ideas with no help

Comments:

Student or Team: _____

Assignment: _____

Directions: Mark the appropriate rating for each criterion. Use these individual ratings to assign an overall rating for the assignment.

RATINGS	0 Working on it!	1 Novice	2 Acceptable	3 Out of the Box!	Not Applicable
OVERALL					

Comments:

ecology	exploration	culture
ecosystems	food chains	weather
customs	traditions	hierarchy
solar system	Braille	metric

Use information from the Web site below to answer the following questions:
http://www.enchantedlearning.com/subjects/astronomy/planets/

1. How many million miles is Mercury from Earth?

2. How much hotter does it get on Venus than Mercury?

3. How long is a year on Venus?

4. How many Earth days does it take for one side of Venus to have both a day and night? About how many years is that?

5. What is the diameter of Mars?

6. About how many days pass on Jupiter in one week on Earth?

7. Which planets have rings? (Jupiter, Saturn, Neptune)

8. Which planet has the most moons?

9. Which planet has the longest year?

10. Create five more questions using the information from the Web site.

Challenge:
Create a chart showing the same information about each planet. Some information you can gather about each planet could include:
- the length of a day (compared to Earth time)
- the length of a year (compared to Earth time)
- the distance from the sun
- the size of the planet
- the number of moons the planet has

Attachment 7   Flashlight Examination

Instructions

Answer the following questions as you examine the flashlight. Use another piece of paper for your answers.

1. Write down your predictions of what will be inside the flashlight. Draw a picture of what you think the inside of the flashlight will look like.

2. Write a short explanation of how you think the flashlight works.

3. Disassemble the flashlight. Draw a picture and label each part of the flashlight.

4. Write about each part of the flashlight. Determine the function of each part.

5. Are there any improvements you could make to this flashlight? If so, describe them.

6. Are there any parts of the flashlight that are unnecessary? If so, tell why and describe how the flashlight would function without them.

7. What purpose does the shiny area around the bulb serve?

8. Write a paragraph telling what you learned by taking apart the flashlight.

© Prufrock Press Inc.

Attachment 8   Electrical Circuit

Instructions

1. Gather a piece of the holiday light string, one piece of duct tape, and a 9-volt battery.

2. Use duct tape to secure one end of the wire to one terminal on the 9-volt battery.

3. Touch the loose wire to the other terminal of the battery. The bulb should light. If it doesn't, make sure the duct tape is securely holding the other end of the wire on the other terminal.

4. Draw a picture of your completed circuit below. Be sure to label all the parts.

Instructional Materials
- metal cake or sheet pan
- hot tap water
- ice cubes
- large glass jar

Instructions

1. Fill a metal cake pan with ice. Wait a few minutes until the pan gets cold.

2. Pour 2-3 inches of hot tap water into a large glass jar. (Only the teacher may perform this step.)

3. Set the pan of ice on the jar rim and watch what happens.

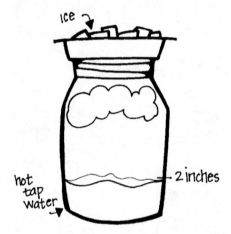

The hot tap water will evaporate, causing water vapor to fill the jar. When the air rises it will run into the cool air at the top of the jar from the metal pan. The cool air will cause the water vapor to condense on the side of the jar and the bottom of the pan.

**Crater Found Near Yucatan
Peninsula
By M. Pact Syte**

Scientists recently discovered a large crater near the tip of the Yucatan Peninsula in the Gulf of Mexico. They estimate the crater to be around 65 million years old. Scientists know the impact would have caused an enormous blast, fires, acid rain, and eventually an ice age. They wonder how any life was able to survive after the impact.

**Scientists Discover K-T Layer of Clay
By Terra Digger**
Scientists in Italy discovered unusual levels of iridium, a rare element existing mainly in space, in a layer of clay. The layer of clay has since been discovered in many places around Earth. In each area, the clay contains the high levels of iridium. Scientists are puzzled by the high levels of iridium and do not know what to think about the layer of clay being deposited all around the Earth. They are working to discover how high levels of iridium could be deposited all around Earth.

**Another K-T Discovery
By Dinah Sore**
After the recent discovery of the K-T layer of clay, paleontologists began to notice that all dinosaur fossils being uncovered were below the layer of clay. They don't know of any dinosaur fossils that have been discovered above the layer. Scientists are wondering what this information could mean. They believe this layer of clay and the extinction of the dinosaurs are directly related.

The **scientific method** is a process developed by scientists to learn more about the world. In simplest terms, the scientific method is about asking questions, observing, making guesses, testing guesses, and trying to develop a theory.

There are four main steps in the scientific method. **Observation** is the first step. When we observe something, we use our five senses to make sense of it. During this step in the scientific method, scientists ask many questions about what they are observing. An example would be a scientist observing water beads on the outside of a glass. The question might be, "I wonder why there's water on the outside of the glass?"

The next step in the scientific method is to develop a **hypothesis**. A hypothesis is a possible explanation for the observation. There may be many hypotheses for one observation. In the example above, a hypothesis might be that the glass was leaking or got wet when water sprayed on it.

The third step in the scientific method is **prediction**. Scientists develop testable predictions about their hypotheses. Testable means the scientists will be able to create an experiment to test the hypothesis. In the example above, the scientist might develop a test in which he or she would dry the glass and fill it with water again to observe whether it would leak again.

The final step in the scientific method is to perform the **experiment**. An experiment helps prove or disprove the hypothesis. In the wet glass experiment, if a scientist discovers that water doesn't leak through the glass, he or she would choose another hypothesis. Then the scientist would again develop another testable prediction and perform an experiment to test the hypothesis.

When a scientist develops a hypothesis, makes a testable prediction, performs an experiment, and discovers that the hypothesis is correct, he or she must repeat the experiment many times. If the experiment produces the same results each time, then the hypothesis becomes a **theory**. A theory is a hypothesis that has been proven many times by many scientists.

Read a biography or autobiography about a famous person that you want to learn more about. Then complete a tic-tac-toe in any direction by completing three of these activities during independent study. Lightly shade in the boxes as you complete each task.

Write	**Model**	**Math**
Write a report about the famous person. What important contributions did this person make to society?	Make a pyramid to show the major contribution this person made. (Use the paper pyramid pattern on Attachment 13.)	Collect at least ten numeric facts about your famous person. For example: date of birth, country of birth, number of elections won, etc.
Survey	**Portrait**	**Compare**
Take a survey of opinions on an interesting question related to this famous person. For example: On a scale from one to ten, how well known do you think this person is?	Draw a portrait of this famous person.	Compare the person you read about to Louis Braille and/or Helen Keller. Look for ways they are alike or different.
Fact File	**Research**	**Teach**
Collect interesting facts about the person you are learning about. Decide how many facts you want to collect and how you will display them.	List ten facts about the time is history that your famous person lived. Share what you find out with the group in an interesting way.	Prepare and teach a lesson about this famous person.

Bonus: Create a collage that symbolizes what the famous person's life is/was about. Cut out pictures from magazines and newspapers that remind you of some aspect of that person's life.

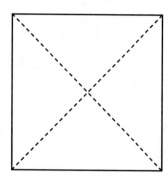

1. Begin with a square piece of paper.

2. Fold the square in half as shown, creating 2 creases.

3. Unfold the square and cut from one corner to the center fold.

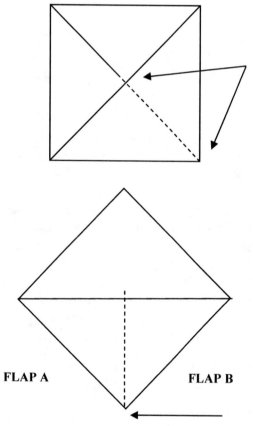

FLAP A   FLAP B

4. Fold Flap B under Flap A to create a three-dimensional triangular pyramid. Secure with glue or tape.

5. You can create a four-sided pyramid by making 4 paper pyramids and gluing the backsides together.

Systems Book 1
Vocabulary and Materials Checklist

Activity	Vocabulary	Materials Needed
1		1 copy of Attachment 5 per pair of students journal for each student
2	galaxy gravity solar system universe	computer with Internet access 5 pieces of chart paper 1 copy of Attachment 6 per student books about space, space exploration, and the moon
3	Louis Braille multilingual	computer with Internet access biographies of Helen Keller and Louis Braille journals
4	circuit conductor innovation insulator invention discovery	several flashlights that can be disassembled and reassembled 1 working string of holiday lights (See Preparation.) (6) 9-volt batteries duct tape wire strippers wire cutters several items to test the ability to conduct electricity (cotton ball, penny, scissors, ruler, water, paper clip, etc.) copies of Attachments 7 and 8 (as needed) computer with Internet access **Optional:** 1 large, used box several feet of insulated wire
5	characteristics landforms regional	books about your state journals computer with Internet access
6	metric prefix	string several sets of Cuisenaire Rods or the centimeter cubes and rods torn from the back of a consumable math book rulers journals
7	celadon shard trades	multiple matching copies of *A Single Shard* book, by Linda Sue Park journals
8	detrimental locomotive structure	several social studies textbooks focusing on your state's history computer with Internet access journals

9	customary preserve traditional	computer with Internet access books about customs and celebrations in your state
10	ancient generation legends myths	journals computers
11	condensation evaporation molecules precipitation accumulation water vapor	several bowls water clear jar with a lid ice cubes **Optional:** hot plate small pan with water
12	photosynthesis carnivores herbivores omnivores producers primary consumers secondary consumers decomposers	books from the library about food chains and food webs journals computer with Internet access
13	atmosphere weather	computer with Internet access books about weather
14	adapt ecosystem habitat	computer with Internet access books about different ecosystems, plants, and animals
15	demise iridium mass extinction meteorite	copies of Attachments 10 and 11 (as needed) books and references about dinosaurs and their extinction computer with Internet access journals
16		1 copy of Attachment 5 per student journals

Note: Paper and pencils should be on hand each day, as should writing and illustration supplies, and may not be listed on the checklist

Systems Book 1
Differentiation Strategies and TEKS Checklist

Activity	Differentiation Strategies	TEKS: Language Arts and Reading	TEKS: Mathematics	TEKS: Social Studies	TEKS: Science
1	**Knowledge and Skills** • Categorizing • Attributes **Multiple Perspectives** • Brainstorming				

Activity	Differentiation Strategies	TEKS: Language Arts and Reading	TEKS: Mathematics	TEKS: Social Studies	TEKS: Science
2	**Analysis and Synthesis** • Generalizations • Critical Thinking	Demonstrate effective communications skills that reflect such demands as interviewing, reporting, requesting, and providing information	Use place value to read, write, compare, and order whole numbers through the millions place		Identify and describe the roles of some organisms in living systems such as plants in a schoolyard, and parts in nonliving systems such as a light bulb in a circuit
			Use addition and subtraction to solve problems involving whole numbers		
	Multiple Perspectives • Inquiry	Form and revise questions for investigations, including questions arising from interests and units of study			Predict and draw conclusions about what happens when part of a system is removed
	Methodology and Use of Resources • Uses Technological Media • Note Taking	Use multiple sources, including electronic texts, experts, and print resources, to locate information relevant to research questions	Use multiplication to solve problems involving two digit numbers		Identify patterns of change such as in weather, metamorphosis, and objects in the sky
			Use division to solve problems involving one digit divisors		
		Produce research projects and reports in effective formats using visuals to support meaning, as appropriate	Select or develop an appropriate problem-solving strategy, including drawing a picture, looking for a pattern, systematic guessing and checking, acting it out, making a table, working a simpler problem, or working backwards to solve a problem		
		Use compiled information and knowledge to raise additional, unanswered questions			
		Write to inform such as to explain, describe, report, and narrate	Use tools such as real objects, manipulatives, and technology to solve problems		
3	**Knowledge and Skills**	Read for varied purposes such as to be informed, to be	The student is expected to locate and name points on a	Organize and interpret information in outlines,	

Activity	Differentiation Strategies	TEKS: Language Arts and Reading	TEKS: Mathematics	TEKS: Social Studies	TEKS: Science
	• Attributes **Analysis and Synthesis** • Generalizations • Inferences • Evaluate Situations **Communication** • Uses Technological Media	entertained, to appreciate the writer's craft, and to discover models for his/her own writing Use his/her own knowledge and experience to comprehend Paraphrase and summarize text to recall, inform, and organize ideas Draw inferences such as conclusions or generalizations and support them with text evidence and experience Represent text information in different ways such as in outline, timeline, or graphic organizer Use multiple sources, including electronic texts, experts, and print resources, to locate information relevant to research questions	number line using whole numbers, fractions such as halves and fourths, and decimals such as tenths Identify the mathematics in everyday situations	reports, databases, and visuals including graphs, charts, timelines, and maps	
4	**Knowledge and Skills** • Attributes • Categorizing • Research	Read for varied purposes such as to be informed, to be entertained, to appreciate the writer's craft, and to discover models for his/her own	Measure to solve problems involving length (including perimeter), weight, capacity, time, temperature, and area	Describe the contributions of famous inventors and scientists such as Gail Borden, Joseph Glidden, and Patillo Higgins and	Demonstrate safe practices during field and laboratory investigation Collect information by

Activity	Differentiation Strategies	TEKS: Language Arts and Reading	TEKS: Mathematics	TEKS: Social Studies	TEKS: Science
	Analysis and Synthesis • SCAMPER • Drawing Conclusions • Generalizations	writing Represent text in different ways such as in outline, timeline, or graphic organizer Form and revise questions for investigations, including questions arising from interest and units of study Summarize and organize information from multiple sources by taking notes, outlining ideas, and making charts	Graph a given set of data using an appropriate graphical representation such as a picture or line	their contributions Create written and visual material such as journal entries, reports, graphic organizers, outlines, and bibliographies Express ideas orally based on research and experience	observing and measuring Communicate valid conclusions Connect Grade 4 science concepts with the history of science and contributions of scientists Predict and draw conclusions about when a part of a system is removed Conduct tests, compare data, and draw conclusions about physical properties of matter including states of matter, conduction, density, and buoyancy

70

Activity	Differentiation Strategies	TEKS: Language Arts and Reading	TEKS: Mathematics	TEKS: Social Studies	TEKS: Science
5	**Analysis and Synthesis** • Drawing Conclusions **Multiple Perspectives** • Inquiry **Methodology and Use of Resources** • Note Taking • Research	Distinguish between the speaker's opinion and verifiable fact Draw inferences such as conclusions or generalizations and support them with text evidence and experience Represent text information in different ways such as in outline, timeline, or graphic organizer Interpret text ideas through such varied means as journal writing, discussion, enactment, media Connect, compare, and contrast ideas, themes, and issues across text Use multiple sources, including electronic texts, experts, and print resources, to locate information relevant to research questions Summarize and organize information gathered by taking notes, outlining ideas, or making charts	Graph a given set of data using an appropriate graphical representation such as a picture or line Identify the mathematics in everyday situations	Apply geographic tools, including grid systems, legends, symbols, scales, and compass roses, to construct and interpret maps Translate geographic data into a variety of formats such as raw data to graphs and maps Compare the regions Texas (your state) with regions of the United States and other parts of the world Describe a variety of regions in Texas (your state) and the Western Hemisphere such as landform, climate, and vegetation regions that result from physical characteristics	

71

Activity	Differentiation Strategies	TEKS: Language Arts and Reading	TEKS: Mathematics	TEKS: Social Studies	TEKS: Science
6	**Analysis and Synthesis** • Generalizations • Drawing Conclusions • Evaluation	Describe how the author's point of view affects the text Write to entertain such as to compose humorous poems or short stories	The student is expected to measure to solve problems involving length, including perimeter, time, temperature and area Estimate and measure weight using standard units including ounces, pounds, grams, and kilograms Estimate and measure capacity using standard units including milliliters, liters, cups, pints, quarts, and gallons Use place value to read, write, compare, and order decimals involving tenths and hundredths, including money, using concrete models Generate equivalent fractions using concrete and pictorial models Use multiplication to solve problems involving two-digit numbers Identify the mathematics in everyday situations		

72

Activity	Differentiation Strategies	TEKS: Language Arts and Reading	TEKS: Mathematics	TEKS: Social Studies	TEKS: Science
7	**Innovation and Application** • Flexibility **Analysis and Synthesis** • Generalizations **Communication** • Research **Relevance and Significance** • Field Lesson • Resource Person	Paraphrase and summarize text to recall, inform, and organize ideas Draw inferences such as conclusions or generalizations and support them with text evidence and experience Answer different types and levels of questions such as open-ended, literal, and interpretive as well as test-like questions such as multiple choice, true-false, and short answer Offer observations, make connections, react, speculate, interpret, and raise questions in response to texts Connect, compare, and contrast ideas, themes, and issues across text Describe how the author's perspective or point of view affects the text Use multiple sources, including electronic texts, experts, and print resources, to locate information relevant			

Activity	Differentiation Strategies	TEKS: Language Arts and Reading	TEKS: Mathematics	TEKS: Social Studies	TEKS: Science
		to research questions Determine distinctive and common characteristics of cultures through wide reading Articulate and discuss themes and connections that cross cultures Write to inform such as to explain, describe, report, and narrate			

74

Activity	Differentiation Strategies	TEKS: Language Arts and Reading	TEKS: Mathematics	TEKS: Social Studies	TEKS: Science
8	**Analysis and Synthesis** • Evaluate Situations **Multiple Perspectives** • Point of View **Communication** • Creative Writing • Research	Draw inferences such as conclusions or generalizations and support them with text evidence and experience Use multiple sources, including electronic texts, experts, and print resources, to locate information relevant to research questions		Describe how scientific discoveries and technological innovations have benefited individuals, businesses, and society in Texas (your state) Predict how future scientific discoveries and technological innovations might affect life in Texas (your state) Identify the impact of railroads on life in Texas (your state), including changes to cities and major industries Identify ways in which technological changes have resulted in increased interdependence among Texas (your state), the United States, and the world Explain how developments in transportation and communication have influenced economic activities in Texas (your state)	

Activity	Differentiation Strategies	TEKS: Language Arts and Reading	TEKS: Mathematics	TEKS: Social Studies	TEKS: Science
9	**Knowledge and Skills** • Research • Inquiry • Observation **Communication** • Demonstration **Relevance and Significance** • Resource Person	Represent text information in different ways such as in outline, timeline, or graphic organizer Interpret text ideas through such varied means as journal writing, discussion, enactment, media Connect, compare, and contrast ideas, themes, and issues across text Use multiple sources, including electronic texts, experts, and print resources, to locate information relevant to research questions Summarize and organize information gathered by taking notes, outlining ideas, or making charts		Identify customs, celebrations, and traditions of various culture groups in Texas (your state) Describe the location of cities in Texas (your state) and explain their distribution, past and present Organize and interpret information in outlines, reports, databases, and visuals including graphs, charts, timelines, and maps Create written and visual material such as journal entries, reports, graphic organizers, outlines, and bibliographies	
10	**Knowledge and Skills** • Inquiry **Analysis and Synthesis** • Generalizations	Determine the purposes for listening such as to gain information, to solve problems, or to enjoy and appreciate Interpret speakers' messages (both verbal and nonverbal), purposes, and perspectives		Identify customs, celebrations, and traditions of various culture groups in the development of Texas (your state)	

Activity	Differentiation Strategies	TEKS: Language Arts and Reading	TEKS: Mathematics	TEKS: Social Studies	TEKS: Science
	Methodology and Use of Resources • Note Taking • Resource Person • Research	Connect his/her own experiences, information, insights, and ideas with those of others through speaking and listening Demonstrate effective communications skills that reflect such demands as interviewing, reporting, requesting, and providing information Write to express, discover, record, develop, reflect on ideas, and to problem solve			
11	**Analysis and Synthesis** • Generalizations • Evaluation **Multiple Perspectives** • Shared Inquiry **Communication** • Demonstration • Uses Technological Media	Draw inferences such as conclusions or generalizations and support them with text evidence and experience Use multiple sources, including electronic texts, experts, and print resources, to locate information relevant to research questions Represent text information in different ways such as in outline, timeline, or graphic organizer Interpret text ideas through	The student is expected to measure to solve problems involving length, including perimeter, time, temperature and area Use division to solve problems with one-digit divisors	Identify patterns of change such as in weather, metamorphosis, and objects in the sky Identify the Sun as the major source of energy for the Earth and understand its role in the growth of plants, in the creation of winds, and in the water cycle Predict and draw conclusions about what happens when part of a system is removed	

Activity	Differentiation Strategies	TEKS: Language Arts and Reading	TEKS: Mathematics	TEKS: Social Studies	TEKS: Science
		such varied means as journal writing, discussion, enactment, media Write to inform such as to explain, describe, report, and narrate			

Activity	Differentiation Strategies	TEKS: Language Arts and Reading	TEKS: Mathematics	TEKS: Social Studies	TEKS: Science
12	**Knowledge and Skills** • Sequencing • Inquiry **Analysis and Synthesis** • Drawing Conclusions • Generalizations • Critical Thinking **Communication** • Research	Demonstrate effective communications skills that reflect such demands as interviewing, reporting, requesting, and providing information Give precise directions and instructions such as in games and tasks Form and revise questions for investigations, including questions arising from interests and units of study Write to inform such as to explain, describe, report, and narrate Use multiple sources, including electronic texts, experts, and print resources, to locate information relevant to research questions Produce research projects and reports in effective formats using visuals to support meaning, as appropriate Use compiled information and knowledge to raise additional, unanswered questions			Represent the natural world using models and identify their limitations Collect and analyze information using tools including calculators, safety goggles, microscopes, cameras, sound recorders, computers, hand lenses, rulers, thermometers, meter sticks, timing devices, balances, and compasses Identify and describe the roles of some organisms in living systems such as plants in a schoolyard, and parts in nonliving systems such as a light bulb in a circuit Predict and draw conclusions about what happens when part of a system is removed Identify the Sun as the major source of energy for the Earth and understand its role in the growth of plants, in the creation of winds, and in the water cycle

Activity	Differentiation Strategies	TEKS: Language Arts and Reading	TEKS: Mathematics	TEKS: Social Studies	TEKS: Science
13	**Knowledge and Skills** • Attributes • Categorizing • Observation **Analysis and Synthesis** • Generalizations • Drawing Conclusions **Methodology and Use of Resources** • Resource Person • Research	Demonstrate effective communications skills that reflect such demands as interviewing, reporting, requesting, and providing information Use multiple sources, including electronic texts, experts, and print resources, to locate information relevant to research questions Produce research projects and reports in effective formats using visuals to support meaning, as appropriate Write to inform such as to explain, describe, report, and narrate	Identify the mathematics in everyday situations Make generalizations from patterns or sets of examples and nonexamples	Analyze information by sequencing, categorizing, identifying cause-and-effect relationships, comparing, contrasting, finding the main idea, summarizing, making generalizations and predictions, and drawing inferences and conclusions Organize and interpret information in outlines, reports, databases, and visuals including graphs, charts, timelines, and maps Express ideas orally based on research and experience Create written and visual material such as journal entries, reports, graphic organizers, outlines, and bibliographies	Identify patterns of change such as in weather, metamorphosis, and objects in the sky

Activity	Differentiation Strategies	TEKS: Language Arts and Reading	TEKS: Mathematics	TEKS: Social Studies	TEKS: Science
14	**Knowledge and Skills** • Attributes • Demonstration **Analysis and Synthesis** • Generalizations • Drawing Conclusions • Evaluate Situations	Demonstrate effective communications skills that reflect such demands as interviewing, reporting, requesting, and providing information Use multiple sources, including electronic texts, experts, and print resources, to locate information relevant to research questions Produce research projects and reports in effective formats using visuals to support meaning, as appropriate Use compiled information and knowledge to raise additional, unanswered questions Write to inform such as to explain, describe, report, and narrate	Identify the mathematics in everyday situations Interpret bar graphs	Analyze information by sequencing, categorizing, identifying cause-and-effect relationships, comparing, contrasting, finding the main idea, summarizing, making generalizations and predictions, and drawing inferences and conclusions Organize and interpret information in outlines, reports, databases, and visuals including graphs, charts, timelines, and maps Express ideas orally based on research and experience Create written and visual material such as journal entries, reports, graphic organizers, outlines, and bibliographies	Construct simple graphs, tables, maps, and charts to organize, examine, and evaluate information Represent the natural world using models and identify their limitations Describe the roles of some organisms in living systems such as plants in a schoolyard, and parts in nonliving systems such as a light bulb in a circuit Predict and draw conclusions about what happens when part of a system is removed Identify characteristics that allow members within a species to survive and reproduce Compare adaptive characteristics of various species

Activity	Differentiation Strategies	TEKS: Language Arts and Reading	TEKS: Mathematics	TEKS: Social Studies	TEKS: Science
	Analysis and Synthesis • Drawing Conclusions	Find similarities and differences across texts such as in treatment, scope, or organization			Analyze and interpret information to construct reasonable explanations from direct and indirect evidence
	Ethics/Unanswered Questions • Provocative Questions	Offer observations, make connections, react, speculate, interpret, and raise questions in response to text			Communicate valid conclusions Analyze, review, and critique scientific explanations, including hypotheses and theories, as to their strengths and weaknesses using scientific evidence and information
	Multiple Perspectives • Shared Inquiry	Write to inform such as to explain, describe, report, and narrate			Evaluate the impact of research on scientific thought, society, and the environment
15	**Relevance and Significance** • Group Consensus	Draw conclusions about "what happened before" using fossils or charts and tables			Predict and draw conclusions about what happens when part of a system is removed Identify the kinds of species that lived in the past and compare them to existing species

Activity	Differentiation Strategies	TEKS: Language Arts and Reading	TEKS: Mathematics	TEKS: Social Studies	TEKS: Science
16	**Knowledge and Skills** • Attributes • Categorizing **Multiple Perspectives** • Brainstorming				

Systems
National Standards Checklist

Activity	Language Arts and Reading	Mathematics	Social Studies	Science
1	Uses prewriting strategies to plan written work Uses strategies to write for a variety of purposes Contributes to group discussions Listens to classmates and adults	Understands that data come in many different forms and that collecting, organizing, and displaying data can be done in many ways		

84

Activity	Language Arts and Reading	Mathematics	Social Studies	Science
2	Uses prewriting strategies to plan written work Uses strategies to write for a variety of purposes Writes narrative accounts, such as poems and stories Uses a variety of strategies to plan research Uses strategies to gather and record information for research topics Uses strategies to compile information into written reports or summaries Knows the defining characteristics of a variety of literary forms and genres Understands techniques used to convey messages in visual media	Adds, subtracts, multiplies, and divides whole numbers and decimals Adds and subtracts simple fractions Understands the basic measures perimeter, area, volume, capacity, mass, angle, and circumference Understands that measurement is not exact	Geography Understands the spatial organization of places through such concepts as location, distance, direction, scale, movement, and region	Knows that night and day are caused by the Earth's rotation on its axis Knows that the Earth is one of several planets that orbit the Sun and that the Moon orbits the Earth Knows that the patterns of stars in the sky stay the same, although they appear to slowly move from east to west across the sky nightly and different stars can be seen in different seasons Knows that planets look like stars, but over time they appear to wander among the constellations Knows that telescopes magnify distant objects in the sky Knows that the Earth's gravity pulls any object toward it without touching it
3	Uses prewriting strategies to plan written work	Uses a variety of strategies to understand problem situations	History Knows how to construct time lines in significant historical	Knows that although the same scientific investigation may give slightly different results

Activity	Language Arts and Reading	Mathematics	Social Studies	Science
	Uses a variety of strategies to plan research Uses electronic media to gather and record information for research topics Uses strategies to compile information into written reports or summaries Uses prior knowledge and experience to understand and respond to new information	Recognizes a wide variety of patterns and the rules that explain them	developments that mark at evenly spaced intervals the years, decades, and centuries Understands the origins and changes in methods of writing over time and how the changes made communication and their impact on the spread of ideas Knows about people who have made significant contributions in the field of communications	when it is carried out by different persons, or at different times or places, the general evidence collected from the investigation should be replicable by others Knows that scientists and engineers often work in teams to accomplish a task
4	Writes autobiographical compositions Uses a variety of strategies to plan research Uses strategies to gather and record information for research topics Uses strategies to compile information into written reports or summaries Organizes ideas for oral	Organizes and displays data in simple bar graphs, pie charts, and line graphs	Economics Knows that innovation is the introduction of an invention into a use that has economic value History Distinguishes between past, present, and future Understands that specific individuals had a great impact on history Understands that specific ideas	Knows the organization of a simple electrical circuit Knows that electrically charged material pulls on all other materials and can attract or repel other charged materials Knows that good scientific explanations are based on evidence and scientific knowledge Uses appropriate tools and

Activity	Language Arts and Reading	Mathematics	Social Studies	Science
	presentations Knows the main formats and characteristics of familiar media		had an impact on history Knows about the development of the wheel and its early uses in ancient societies Understands the development and the influence of basic tools on work and behavior Understands the influence of Enlightenment ideas on American society	simple equipment Knows that people of all ages, backgrounds, and groups have made contributions to science and technology throughout history
5	Uses a variety of strategies to plan research Uses strategies to gather and record information for research topics Uses strategies to compile information into written reports or summaries Organizes ideas for oral presentations	Understands that data come in many different forms and that collecting, organizing, and displaying data can be done in many ways	Geography Knows the characteristics of a variety of regions Knows the similarities and differences in characteristics of culture in different regions History Understands major historical events and developments in the state or region that involved interaction among various groups	Knows that scientists and engineers often work in teams to accomplish a task
6	Uses prewriting strategies to plan written work	Understands equivalent forms of basic percents, fractions,		Knows that good scientific explanations are based on

87

Activity	Language Arts and Reading	Mathematics	Social Studies	Science
	Uses strategies to write for a variety of purposes Writes narrative accounts, such as poems and stories Uses strategies to compile information into written reports or summaries Uses conventions of spelling in written compositions	and decimals Adds, subtracts, multiplies, and divides whole numbers and decimals Selects and uses appropriate tools for given measurement situations Understands the basic measures perimeter, area, volume, capacity, mass, angle, and circumference Understands that measurement is not exact Uses specific strategies to estimate quantities and measurements		evidence and scientific knowledge Knows that scientists use different kinds of investigations
7	Writes narrative accounts, such as poems and stories Writes in response to literature Uses a variety of strategies to plan research			

88

Activity	Language Arts and Reading	Mathematics	Social Studies	Science
	Uses a variety of strategies to plan research			
	Uses strategies to gather and record information for research topics			
	Establishes a purpose for reading			
	Understands author's purpose			
	Understands similarities and differences within and among literary works from various genre and cultures			
	Uses a variety of verbal communication skills			

Activity	Language Arts and Reading	Mathematics	Social Studies	Science
	Uses strategies to edit and publish written work		Geography Understands how changing transportation and communication technology have affected relationships between locations	Knows that people of all ages, backgrounds, and groups have made contributions to science and technology throughout history
	Uses strategies to write for a variety of purposes			
	Uses a variety of strategies to plan research		Understands how regions change over time and the consequences of these changes	Knows that although people using scientific inquiry have learned much about the objects, events, and phenomena in nature, science is an ongoing process and will never be finished
	Uses strategies to gather and record information for research topics		Knows the causes and effects of human migration	
8	Uses electronic media to gather and record information for research topics		Knows the major transportation routes that link resources with consumers and transportation modes used	Knows that scientists and engineers often work in teams to accomplish a task
			Knows about the forced relocation of Native Americans and how their lives, rights, and territories were affected by European colonization and expansion of the U.S.	
			Knows the developments in rail transportation beginning in the 19th century and the effects of national systems of railroad transport on the lives of people	

Activity	Language Arts and Reading	Mathematics	Social Studies	Science
	Uses strategies to edit and publish written work		Geography	
			Knows the similarities and differences in characteristics of culture in different regions	
	Uses strategies to write for a variety of purposes			
			Knows how humans adapt to variations in the physical environment	
	Uses a variety of strategies to plan research			
	Uses electronic media to gather and record information for research topics		Knows how communities benefit from physical environment	
9			History	
	Uses strategies to gather and record information for research topics		Knows how to construct time lines in significant historical developments that mark at evenly spaced intervals the years, decades, and centuries	
	Understands the author's purpose			
			Knows how to identify patterns of change and continuity in the history of the community, state, and nation, and in the lives of people of various cultures from times long ago until today	
	Knows that a variety of people are involved in the creation of media messages and products			
			Understands the broadly defined eras of state and local historical events	

91

Activity	Language Arts and Reading	Mathematics	Social Studies	Science
			Knows the ways that families long ago expressed and transmitted their beliefs and values through oral tradition, literature, songs, art, religion, community celebrations, mementos, food, and language	
10	Uses strategies to edit and publish written work Evaluates own and others' writing Uses strategies to write for different audiences Writes narrative accounts, such as poems and stories Writes autobiographical compositions Writes personal letters Uses electronic media to gather and record information for research topics Uses multiple		History Knows how to interpret data presented in time lines Distinguishes between past, present, and future time Knows the ways that families long ago expressed and transmitted their beliefs and values through oral tradition, literature, songs, art, religion, community celebrations, mementos, food, and language Understands how stories, legends, songs, ballads, games, and tall tales describe the environment, lifestyles, beliefs, and struggles of people in various regions of the country Understands various aspects of	

Activity	Language Arts and Reading	Mathematics	Social Studies	Science
	representations of information Organizes ideas for oral presentations		family life, structures, and roles in different cultures and in many eras	
11	Uses prewriting strategies to plan written work Evaluates own and others' writing Uses electronic media to gather and record information for research topics Uses strategies to gather and record information for research topics	Adds, subtracts, multiplies, and divides whole numbers and decimals Understands the basic measures perimeter, area, volume, capacity, mass, angle, and circumference Selects and uses appropriate tools for given measurement situations		Knows that water exists in the air in different forms and changes from one form to another through various processes Knows that most of Earth's surface is covered by water, that most of that water is salt water in oceans and that fresh water is found in rivers, lakes, underground sources, and glaciers

93

Activity	Language Arts and Reading	Mathematics	Social Studies	Science
12	Uses electronic media to gather and record information for research topics Uses strategies to gather and record information for research topics		Geography Knows the components of ecosystems at a variety of scales Knows ways in which humans can change ecosystems Knows plants and animals associated with various vegetation and climatic regions on Earth	Knows that the Sun provides light and heat necessary to maintain the temperature of the Earth Knows the organization of simple food chains and food webs Knows that an organism's patterns of behavior are related to the nature of that organism's environment
13	Uses strategies to edit and publish written work Uses electronic media to gather and record information for research topics Uses multiple representations of information to find information for research topics	Understands that statistical predictions are better for describing what proportion of a group will experience something rather then which individuals within the group will experience something, and how often events will occur rather than exactly when they will occur	Geography Knows the physical components of Earth's atmosphere Knows how Earth's position relative to the Sun affects events and conditions on Earth	Plans and conducts simple investigations, depending on the questions they are trying to answer Uses appropriate tools and simple equipment to gather scientific data and extend the senses

Activity	Language Arts and Reading	Mathematics	Social Studies	Science
14	Uses strategies to edit and publish written word Uses a variety of strategies to plan research Uses electronic media to gather and record information for research topics Organizes ideas for oral presentation	Organizes and displays data in simple bar graphs, pie charts, and line graphs	Knows the components of ecosystems at a variety of scales Knows ways in which humans can change ecosystems Knows plants and animals associated with various vegetation and climatic regions on Earth	Knows that fossils provide evidence about the plants and animals that lived long ago and the nature of the environment at that time Knows that an organism's patterns of behavior are related to the nature of that organism's environment Knows that changes in the environment can have different effects on different organisms
15	Uses strategies to edit and publish written word Uses a variety of strategies to plan research Uses electronic media to gather and record information for research topics	Understands that data represent specific pieces of information about real-world objects or activities Understands that statistical predictions are better for describing what proportion of a group will experience something rather then which individuals within the group will experience something, and how often events will occur rather than exactly when they will occur	Geography Knows the basic elements of maps and globes Understands that "chance events" had an impact on history	Knows that fossils provide evidence about the plants and animals that lived long ago and the nature of the environment at that time Knows that good scientific explanations are based on evidence (observations) and scientific knowledge
16	Uses prewriting strategies to plan written work			